GETTING OLD
is not for
SISSIES

GETTING OLD
is not for
SISSIES

Memoir of a Caregiver

by

Anne E. Smith

XULON PRESS

Xulon Press
2301 Lucien Way #415
Maitland, FL 32751
407.339.4217
www.xulonpress.com

Unless otherwise indicated, Scripture quotations taken from the New King James Version (NKJV). Copyright © 1982 by Thomas Nelson, Inc. Used by permission. All rights reserved.

Printed in the United States of America.

ISBN-13: 978-1-54562-997-0

In memory of Doris Fisher
"Dusty"

"We don't grieve without first loving, and we
don't love without gaining more than we could
ever lose."
–Author unknown

Contents

Introduction

In the spring of 2012, my sister-in-law, Nina, asked me if I would help care for her eighty-four-year-old mother, Dusty, who was in an assisted living facility named Bridgeport. Dusty had been diagnosed with dementia a few years earlier, but needed more care as the disease progressed. The thought of spending eight hours a day in a nursing home facility with someone whom I had just recently met filled me with trepidation, but my husband had passed away three years earlier and my children were grown, so I decided to give it a try. I had *no* experience but learned fairly quickly by asking questions and watching the other caregivers. I had planned to help out just for the summer, but that turned into nearly four years. The first two years were at Bridgeport until Dusty broke her hip. She was then transferred to Creekside, another assisted living facility with a memory care unit for Alzheimer's/dementia patients.

She remained there until her death on June 28, 2016.

Chapter 1

I flew into Annapolis in the beginning of July 2012 and stayed with Tom and Nina, my brother and sister-in-law. Since I had only planned to assist Dusty for the summer, initially I did not have a car and Tom dropped me off at Bridgeport Assisted Living that first morning. While driving together, I shared a few of my concerns and hesitancies, that boiled down to this: I knew next to nothing about dementia and nothing about elder care. Tom listened empathetically, and as we pulled up to the front door he exuded a confidence in me that I didn't have in myself and wished me good luck.

I had only met Dusty for the first time while visiting Tom and Nina the previous fall. Nina made a point to have lunch with Dusty nearly every day, and I accompanied her a few times while I was there. She also brought Dusty to the house as often as possible, especially for Sunday dinner with family and friends. Nina was wonderful in monitoring Dusty's care and she handled the heartbreak of watching her mother slip away and become a shell of her former self with remarkable patience, love, and grace.

When I later inquired why she had asked *me* to come and help, Nina simply said, "Because I saw how you were with her."

Permission was required from the administration of Bridgeport however, since I was not a licensed caregiver, and it was reluctantly granted without proper credentials *only* because I was a family member. Nina and I then made an appointment and met together with the head nurse to discuss my duties.

As we entered into her office, she looked put off by the arrangement, opened a notebook listing the services that were provided for the residents, and coolly proceeded to ask me, "What days will you be here? Are you capable of getting her cleaned up, ready, and dressed in the morning? How about transport? Will you be able to transport her to the dining room and various activities? Can you assist with her meals and bathroom needs?"

After discussing each item on her list, we decided I would have full responsibility of Dusty's personal care Monday through Friday from 7:30 a.m. until 4:00 p.m., with the exception of giving her medications and showers. Since Bridgeport was not my employer, there was no on-the-job-training, but she did allow me to watch the other caregivers for the first few days, and help from staff was readily available if needed.

That first morning at 7:15, I went up to Dusty's room on the second floor and was shocked at what I saw. The air conditioning was on full blast and the room was freezing. Dusty was asleep, completely naked except for her Depends, and both she and the bed were drenched in urine. I immediately turned off the air conditioner, covered her up with a blanket that I found in the closet, and waited for the morning shift to arrive in order to learn the proper procedures for getting her up.

A team of two pleasant but harried dayshift caregivers bustled in about thirty minutes later. They were apologetic, embarrassed by the deplorable condition in which I had found Dusty, and indignantly complained about the night shift who had obviously "dropped the ball."

I introduced myself, and explained I was Dusty's private caregiver and timidly asked, "Do you mind if I watch to see how you get her up and ready for breakfast?"

"Not at all," one replied as the other left to get clean sheets.

Moving quickly because of the heavy morning workload, they got Dusty out of bed, cleaned up and dressed in a whirlwind of efficiency and appeared genuinely relieved to hand her over to my charge before rushing off to the next room. I felt like a newborn welcomed into an unknown world with a slap and recognized Dusty must have felt the same way. She had just been unceremoniously catapulted from a sound sleep into the new day with bewildering activity and speed. We had both started off our morning with a rude awakening.

Looking at her tenderly, I approached as though an old friend and asked invitingly, "Would you like to go to breakfast together?"

She nodded in agreement, so we headed off to the dining room at a much slower and less frenzied pace.

While assisting her with her breakfast, the thought came to me: *What could I be doing more important than this?*

I reflected on the parable of the Good Samaritan, which speaks of loving our neighbor as ourselves, and asks in Luke 10:29, "Who *is* my neighbor?"

The progression of my thoughts brought me to this conclusion: We can't help everyone, but our responsibility lies in not looking the other way when someone crosses our path that we can help. Dusty had crossed my path, and I couldn't think of anything more important.

Thus began a journey that changed and enriched my life in ways that I never could have imagined.

Chapter 2

Our Daily Routine

After observing the procedures and techniques of the staff for the first few days, I was on my own. I quickly discovered maneuvering every task into a good idea simplified our daily routine. In other words, each obstacle was met without resistance *if* Dusty agreed it was a good idea, or *if* it was her idea in the first place.

The fact that she hated getting up in the morning was overcome by waking her gently, and saying, "Would you like to have breakfast together?"

We would arrive at a conclusively favorable agreement at the mention of orange juice, and I merely assisted as *she* decided to get up.

We then *walked* to the bathroom instead of opting for the easier wheelchair method because strengthening muscles and getting the circulation going in her feet and legs was a good idea as well. The benefits of regular exercise and negative consequences of inactivity were succinctly summed up by my light-hearted admonishment, "If you don't move it, you lose it."

Although some days were harder than others, it was a concept that she understood and we moved quickly into the bathroom where she could sit down while getting ready.

"You're in the lap of luxury," I frequently kidded while I sponge bathed her and rubbed lotion on her feet, legs, and arms before getting her dressed.

We then moved on to oral hygiene. She didn't like the mouthwash after brushing her teeth, but switching to a less astringent brand helped.

When I asked her afterward, "Don't you feel refreshed and better?" She always said, "Yes."

Once she was clean, dressed, and back in her wheelchair, I gently styled her white hair with a curling iron and commented, "Even though you're as smart as Albert Einstein, I don't want you to look like him."

Next, we made the bed together as a team. She held the pillow while I straightened or changed the sheets and covers. Dusty loved her bright Marimekko bedspread; a company known for its colorful and bold designs. She would often point to it and say, "I love that," and we admired it together every morning before heading to breakfast. Initially, I had no idea that the bedspread would become a focal point of recognition for her and more than anything else, it's what made her room *home*.

After breakfast, we'd walk on the veranda, weather permitting. Once seated in our favorite spot, we sometimes talked or she dozed, but we always held hands and we always enjoyed the view together. At 9:30, we faithfully went to morning exercise class. This idea was at times looked upon with skepticism simply because it required moving from such a comfortable place, but she was generally willing.

One morning, Dusty surprised me. When I mentioned I was tired and didn't feel like going either, she sharply scolded me, "We should go, because it's good for us."

I contritely agreed.

The challenge of getting her to take medications was overcome by the *great* idea of mixing her crushed pills into ice cream. Swallowing whole pills with water is no longer an option with many dementia patients as their ability to understand and even swallow gradually diminishes. The med-tech would initially bring Dusty's crushed medicine in applesauce or a glass of juice. It was problematic though, because if she didn't like the taste or the amount was simply too much, she would refuse to take it. Dusty had a small, delicate appetite and getting her to eat was a challenge that often required creative coaxing. Ice cream, on the other hand, was always received eagerly. Hence, crushed medicine mixed into the first spoonful was a great solution to an otherwise major obstacle. Incredibly, she never once complained about the bitter crunch of the first bite.

Bathroom breaks were on an as-needed basis, but routinely when I got her up in the morning, before lunch and after naps. Sometimes she was able to tell me, but her levels of cognizance varied. In respectfully assisting, she was comforted when I reminded her that it was a function common to all of us.

Throughout the days, we tried to walk as much as possible, changed positions frequently, and got involved in the various morning and afternoon activities: guest musicians, socials, poetry readings, bingo, and crafts. Sometimes she enjoyed them, sometimes she slept through them, and sometimes they annoyed her. I tried to be sensitive to her mood not only for her sake, but mostly to spare others from her loud and unfiltered comments.

If an activity was not to her liking, Dusty would render her verdict, like a judge with a gavel, and loudly declare to all, "This is stupid!"

Other times, she would boldly proclaim that someone was fat. She would say these types of things without wincing—the cause of which I attributed less to dementia, and mostly because I would wince enough for both of us. Avoiding these outbursts, however, became a top priority and I implemented a watchful "distract and run" technique with increasing proficiency. Initially, it was to spare others, but ultimately, to spare me.

A nap after lunch was always a good idea that required no motivation. I would lay her down carefully in bed, making sure she was warm and comfortable, and when I straightened her head on the pillow, I explained, "I don't want you to wake up like a pretzel."

She would laugh and sleepily remind me of the value of a sense of humor while I momentarily sat next to her on the bed while tucking her in. Then, leaning over to kiss her on the forehead, I responded by telling her, "I agree with you; and learning to agree with you has made my life considerably easier."

She laughed again.

While she napped, I would read, sew, or visit other residents. At other times, I ran errands or went home, but I always tried to get her up in time for the afternoon activities.

At 4:00, I took her to dinner. I would get her water, tuck in her napkin, and she decided what she would like to eat by picking one of two entrée choices from the menu. Then with misgivings, I entrusted her to the care of the night shift, hugged her before leaving, and promised to return in the morning.

Chapter 3

What's Left?

The fact Dusty's "filter" had disappeared was by no means only true with Dusty; it was true with many of the residents. It reminded me of a time when my youngest daughter was about two years old. I would pick her up from the babysitter on my way home from work and we would excitedly wait together for the older children to arrive home from school.

One day, as I held her on my lap, she lovingly looked into my face with intense scrutiny and said, "Mommy... (pause)... I wish that I had a big nose just like you!"

I did not know how to respond to that and simply replied with a startled laugh that she had rendered me speechless. Being with the residents was much like that, and trust me, there were many times that I was rendered speechless by their unfiltered comments as well.

With some, it was simply an idiosyncrasy of ageing with its sometimes irascible and less restrained childlike openness. In most cases, though, it stemmed from one of dementia's tragic facets of *unlearning*. Dementia is a broad category of brain diseases, the most common of which is Alzheimer's. In many instances, the regression of an individual is comparable to winding a clock backward to the helplessness of infancy. It is tragic beyond belief because of the gradual long-term damage and inexpressible loss to all involved.

Amazingly though, as much as we are surrounded with sadness from this terrible disease, there were still many moments of lighthearted laughter. The genuine and unpretentious candor of the residents and the enduring attributes that rose above the impairments was the reason for this. It was interesting to witness the memories that didn't fade and to see the inner character traits that still broke through the mental haze. I began to both see and appreciate what was left. I began to love the residents just as they were.

During my days with Dusty, an incongruent sort of normality developed in the midst of abnormal and tumultuous seas. In trying to set a positive tone for the day, I would greet her every morning by cheerfully declaring, "Dusty, we're going to have a good day today."

She would always brighten inquisitively and ask, "Why?"

Sometimes, I would have a special occasion to tell her about, but most often, I would casually reply, "Because if it's not good, we're going to make it good," and we always did.

In caring for her, we not only got into a daily routine, but we truly became friends. It wasn't in the normal sense of the word because nothing with dementia is "normal," but she always noticed they gave her too much food and always asked, "Would you like some?"

When we would walk, I would pull her up from the wheelchair with both hands. She would walk forward and I would walk backward; I became her walker. Together, we would admire the trees and flowers from the veranda.

She would look at me and ask, "Do you know what kind that is?"

I would concede with dismay, "No."

We would try to remember to ask Nina, but we would both forget, and still not know when we would admire them again the next day.

During activities with other residents, if I would inquire about them in conversation, Dusty would comment loudly, "*We* sure are nosey."

She wasn't being critical; it was merely her perception about *us*. If working a puzzle together, I would find the piece that fit, hand it to her, and point out where she should place it. We then both rejoiced in our progress.

She gave me glimpses into her earlier life, when she would thank me for a compliment with regal confidence, yet without vanity or pretense. At times, a memory of home would surface: the architectural genius of Louis Kahn, who built their home, and how light would filter through the window.

Occasionally, a spontaneous Yiddish word would erupt out of nowhere, spoken with laughter.

When I would lay her down in the afternoon for a nap, there was always a tired gratitude in her eyes, and she would softly tell me, "I'm glad you're here."

Once, while getting ready to leave for the evening, Dusty mentioned to me, "I would like to exchange phone numbers with you when we get the chance."

I smiled and told her, "I would be happy to," and thought to myself, *Friends are like that. They keep in touch, spend time together, and are honest.*

When I told her, "I love you," she thanked me and said, "The feeling is mutual."

Chapter 4

Shirley was the one resident that I wanted to avoid because of her blank stare and continuous monotone drone. I always gave her a wide berth when passing her in the parlor and felt dread when one of the staff rolled her out to where Dusty and I sat.

Then, I watched something that changed my point of view. The caregiver introduced her by saying, "This is Shirley; she's my favorite," and explained she had suffered a series of strokes. She then leaned down, and talked with her face to face, caressing her hair as she spoke. A sparkle entered into Shirley's eyes in response to the kindness, like a seedling pushing through hardened ground toward sunshine. She couldn't say my name when we were introduced, but she could say "Shirley" while trying to smile. The strokes had left her imprisoned, and I felt ashamed.

Entering into an assisted living facility, particularly a memory care unit, for the first time can be unnerving with its sights, sounds, and smells, but the "veil of aversion" lifted after my encounter with Shirley. The caregivers' brief explanation of her condition and Shirley's *enlivened* response to compassion enabled me to see the person *within*, and reminded me that hidden behind each diminished exterior was a gifted human being with a story to tell. Vibrant lives from an earlier time emanated from pictures hanging on the walls of their rooms. A happy wedding picture; a handsome young soldier erect with pride before a deployment; a laughing couple, young and in love; family portraits with chubby babies—a past, a history. The residents were once busy parents, talented musicians, engineers, lawyers, and artists that were influential in their various spheres of activity. Several were veterans to whom this country owes a tremendous debt.

One petite woman that I met later at Creekside was a Commander in the Navy. She was an anesthetist nurse with a distinguished military career, including a tour of duty during the Vietnam War in the 1960s. She was one of five innovative women stationed in Saigon who helped turn a ramshackle old apartment building into a US Naval hospital to care for wounded soldiers.

With cleared insight, my initial disinclination vanished and was replaced by humility, admiration, and respect. Quality care in a facility does not happen without good management, training, and sufficient staffing, but the compassion of the caregivers, like the one attending to Shirley that day, are the unsung heroes that make the difference. They are the overworked and underpaid crucial cogs in the complex and ever-expanding industry of elder care.

Chapter 5

Kathryn

One afternoon, Dusty and I went to a poetry reading before dinner. We quietly joined those that had gathered and listened as the activity director read to us from a large open book on her lap. When she had finished, one of the residents began to recite from memory, "If" by Rudyard Kipling, nearly verbatim. She was diminished by frailty and weakened by age, but the words flowed out of her like a refreshing stream, and brought tears to my eyes.

She then proceeded to recount parts of Longfellow's "Song of Hiawatha" again, nearly verbatim. I was captivated not only because they were spoken completely from memory, but also with such emotion.

When everyone dispersed for dinner, I went over to her and briefly introduced Dusty and myself.

She smiled and said, "So nice to meet you both. I'm Kathryn."

I continued by asking, "What inspired your love for poetry?"

She looked at me thoughtfully and responded, "I've always loved it, and many years ago I would read it to my children before tucking them into bed at night."

I could picture the tender scene of her seated at their bedside, and was touched that it would remain a precious life-long memory.

A few days later, we joined Kathryn on the porch. This became a regular occurrence for us where our friendship blossomed and I learned more about her life.

Once, while looking out at the water together, I told her, "You have beautiful eyes."

Without a trace of pride or vanity, my compliment was completely ignored. She unaffectedly remained silent for a few moments, drifting off to when she was a little girl. Her thoughts were disclosed when she finally spoke of a painful childhood memory, recalling her mother's recurrent admonition: "Kathryn, you are *no* follies beauty and therefore need to develop other qualities."

It was an unkind reference, differing her appearance to the beautiful "Ziegfeld Follies" of pre-Broadway New York. Other qualities certainly were developed. She was a voracious reader, an accomplished pianist, and had a doctorate degree, but these many years later, the hurt was still evident as she shook her head and sighed, "What a thing for a mother to say."

One day in early fall, a group of volunteers came to Bridgeport to ensure able and willing residents were registered to vote for the upcoming election in November. This event prompted my question to Kathryn as we walked to the dining room together.

"Are you going to vote?"

"*Of course,*" she responded vehemently.

Continuing on in a milder tone, she explained, "There was only one election that I didn't vote in when I had just become of age. It was right after I was married and I hadn't brought the proper identification. It turned out all right though, because Dewey wasn't elected, and I wasn't going to vote for him anyway."

I thought, *All's well that ends well,* but had to stop and try to figure out: *Who the heck ran against Dewey?* The year was 1948, following the end of World War II, and Truman was reelected by a slim margin. The golden years of economic expansion were just beginning after many years of immeasurable sacrifice, and Kathryn was a young newlywed in hopes of a brighter future. She then shared her father had served in World War I and her husband had served in World War II.

Thoughtfully considering the significant historical timeframe of her life, I questioned, "Do you mind if I ask your age?"

She replied, without trying to be funny, "No, I don't mind at all. I won't tell you, but I don't mind if you ask."

The next time I saw Katherine was at an ice cream social on the porch. These were nice occasions that everyone enjoyed. When the time came, Dusty was still too tired to get up from her nap, so we arrived late and were informed we had just missed it. Since the cleanup was still in process, the activities director kindly salvaged enough ice cream to give us each a cone and we sat down next to Kathryn, who soon chatted away.

She had just returned from lunch with her granddaughter and confided in me with the excitement of a child, "It was like I was a *real* person, and we went to a *real* restaurant."

The pathos of her words was not lost on me, but Kathryn was blissfully unaware and still euphoric from the outing. Looking out over the bay, she continued, "Who could ask for anything better than this?"

She explained to me once again, "My sons found this facility for me," and with great pride she reminded me also once again, "They're both physicians, you know!"

As much as she appreciated being in such a lovely place, she often spoke wistfully of her home and the things that she missed. "Our family would go out on our boat and I would make sandwiches for all of us. We would have such a wonderful time spending the day together on the water."

She then abruptly switched gears from the past to the future, and declared, "I plan to stay here at Bridgeport until next summer, then return home and hire someone to assist with shopping and such."

Her desire was to resume the normal activities of *life before;* and I listened quietly without showing my concern for the low odds of her plan materializing. Her husband had Alzheimer's and had died a year earlier, leaving her alone. Because her sons were busy doctors, they would visit when they could, but when they could wasn't often.

This simply was the way things were, and with unflappable acquiescence, she reminded me, "Aging is better than the alternative."

Still gazing out over the water, she sighed and said, "Getting old is not for sissies."

Kathryn shared with me wisdom, insights, and virtues, some of which were encapsulated by the poetry that she loved.

When I told her how much I always enjoyed visiting with her, she replied, "It's wonderful to have someone who will listen."

It was like discovering gold hidden beneath the earth. Things so precious, yet easily overlooked and unseen beneath the surface of her aged frailty.

Chapter 6

Maria

There was no assigned seating as such in the dining room, but once you sat in a certain spot, it became yours as unequivocally as if you held the title deed to that chair and the property beneath it. Heaven help you, if you took someone else's place.

Maria sat at our table and *owned* the chair to my right. The beverages were generally pre-set before we arrived in the morning, because the servers got to know the residents well. They not only learned everyone's preferences, but more importantly, their food allergies and prescribed dietary restrictions. It was a critical part of their job. Even though I ate breakfast at home, a kind waitress often brought me a glass of orange juice.

One morning, shortly before Maria arrived, I accidently drank her orange juice, thinking it was mine because a glass of cranberry juice was placed at her setting. When she sat down, I promptly learned Maria drinks two juices: a glass of cranberry *and* a glass of orange juice. It was a mistake that one only makes once.

She looked at me with blood-chilling intensity, and said accusingly, in a heavy accent, "You drank *my* juice."

I apologized profusely, replaced it immediately, and learned conclusively that drinking someone else's juice was almost as serious an offence as sitting in someone else's spot. There was no question as to my guilt, and if looks could kill, punishment to the "full extent of the law" would have been achieved.

This incident sparked the beginning of our friendship however, for in my continuing effort to defuse the calamity of my error, I judiciously changed the subject by asking, "Where are you from?"

The tactic worked. Our spiked heart rates decelerated as quickly as they had rocketed only moments before, and she calmly answered as though nothing had happened. "I was born in Czechoslovakia. After the war, I fled from Czechoslovakia to Austria, and then to Germany."

I identified with her plight because of the similar displacement of my own father's family in 1944, when the Nazis invaded Hungary. They too had fled their homeland and eventually immigrated to the United States.

I was intrigued and inquired further, "Why did you go to Germany after the war?"

She lifted her eyes upward and said reverently, "Divine providence led me."

The beauty of a new life for Maria came forth from ashes. It was in post-war Germany, a country in ruins from the Allied bombings, where she met her husband: a handsome American soldier who was stationed there. Incredibly, the simple decision in high school to choose English over French as a second language ultimately steered the course of her life. Had she not been able to communicate in English, her marriage almost certainly wouldn't have happened.

When I asked, "Why did you choose English?"

She replied sternly, "I don't like French!"

As we spent more time together, Maria would fondly reminisce about her husband.

"If he went hunting, I would take a nap in the car. If he went fishing, I would take a nap in the boat."

With a laugh, she shrugged, "At least we were together!"

She and her husband had three children, and were happily married for fifty-eight years before he died. I was utterly amazed at how her consistently stern and rather formidable demeanor would soften whenever she spoke of him.

Chapter 7

Geraldine

To me, Geraldine was the epitome of a sweet little old lady. White soft curls framed her elderly face and gentle blue eyes peered from behind wire-rimmed glasses that often slipped mid-nose. Fragile with age, she had a sweet demeanor, talked softly, and was pleasant. She was a new resident who was escorted to our table and introduced by one of the administrators subsequent to her arrival at Bridgeport. After the manager dropped her off, I tried to calm her "new kid on the block" apprehension by engaging her in conversation.

"Are you married? Do you have any children?"

Geraldine quietly answered, "I was married for fifty-five years before becoming a widow, and have two grown children. I've lived in Annapolis for many years."

"What are your interests and what do you enjoy doing the most?"

She ventured a timid smile and softly said, "I love to read."

Nodding in agreement, I replied, "There are no limitations within the pages of a book."

This shared interest was common ground, but our bond was cemented later, when I gave her some paperbacks by her favorite author, in hopes of making her feel more at home.

The following week, a younger woman walked in with Geraldine at lunch and introduced herself by announcing in a brisk but friendly manner, "I'm Amy, Geraldine's daughter."

She adjusted her mother's chair closer to the table and then, stooping down, put her arm around Geraldine, who was visibly upset.

Amy looked almost embarrassed that Geraldine cried and explained for our benefit the reason for her tears: "Geraldine's house is being rented and much of the furniture sold."

She then clarified the bright side of the situation to her mother once again. "The house still belongs to you, Mom, and all of the meaningful items are being saved in boxes, and stored at my house."

No solace was gained by the clarification. Amy's unmoved expression and Geraldine's recent move to Bridgeport, sadly confirmed, the subject was closed and the decision was final. Then pressed by other matters, Amy gave her mother a quick hug, apologized for not having more time to stay, and hurriedly said, "Goodbye."

When she left, I looked at the sorrow in Geraldine's face with deep sympathy, and said to her tenderly, "Change is hard."

She nodded and replied, "The things that we often talked about are so hard when they're actually here."

"I know," I said, and with a tissue, had to wipe tears not only from her eyes, but mine as well.

Adjusting to her new surroundings was difficult. In loneliness and confusion, she whispered, "I just do what they tell me."

After this, Geraldine's face would brighten every time she saw me, and I continued to offer assistance as we shared our meals together.

One day, after lunch while walking out of the dining room together, I put my arm around her shoulders and informed her, "I'm going to Vermont with family for my first time and I'll be gone for two weeks."

She softly replied, "Your return will give me something to look forward to."

The simple genuineness of her words melted me, and the thought of her selfless sincerity came back to me later.

It was like a taste of friendship in its *purest* form, and its sweetness humbled me.

Chapter 8

Charlie was a lively fellow. He wore a light-weight jacket and baseball cap whether inside or outside, and had a "mischievous school boy" expression that had not diminished with age.

"Do you prefer to be called Charles or Charlie?" I asked.

"I don't care what you call me; just don't call me late for dinner!"

At the weekly social, something unexpected and fun happened. Charlie asked me to dance. Every Friday afternoon, Bridgeport has a social for the residents with refreshments, and music from the

1940s-1960s. Much to my delight, Dusty often snapped her fingers and sang along.

After helping to serve the food and drinks, I sat back down between Dusty and Charlie.

Charlie then asked me, "Would you please crank up the volume on the music?"

"Sure," I replied as I walked over to the boom box and turned it up a couple of notches.

When I returned to my seat, Charlie took me by complete surprise by asking, "Would you like to dance?"

I hesitated ever so slightly, not because I didn't want to, but because of my innate propensity toward bashful inhibition. I overcame that immediately though, and accepted his offer. He then grabbed my hand and I followed him out to the dance floor, where we were the center of attention. As I looked around the room, all—and I mean *all*—eyes were upon us. It was like a suspended, frozen scene from a movie, with jaws dropped, unmoving focused stares, and motionless positions that had stopped mid-air. Charlie put his arm around me, I placed my left hand on his shoulder and held his other hand with my right; then leading the way, he twirled me around as we danced together. Because the afternoon was young, he took turns dancing with others also, but I took pride in being the "trendsetter."

When I later asked, "Charlie, how old are you?" he replied, "You don't want to know!"

Assuring him that I *did* want to know, he reluctantly admitted to being ninety-four years old.

The magic of the moment, however, was everyone in the room was either smiling or laughing; and for that brief moment, it was as if we all felt young again—including me.

Chapter 9

R hoda was a hairdresser who provided service to the residents of Bridgeport on Wednesdays and Fridays. The appointments were handled by families and charged directly to their monthly bill. Remembering appointments and financial transactions were far beyond the capability of most residents, therefore, Rhoda assisted with both.

She knew her elderly customers well and escorted them to and from her tiny one-chair shop in the basement with gentle kindness. The simple act of shampooing and styling the residents' hair was wonderfully restorative and as a result, many compliments were lavished upon them throughout the day.

Dusty's short hair was washed regularly when she was showered, but I would schedule an appointment with Rhoda whenever she needed a trim. Together, Dusty and I would take the elevator to the basement at the prearranged time, and in one smooth motion, Rhoda and I would transfer her from the wheelchair to the salon chair. I would then sit in Dusty's vacant wheelchair nearby and watch as Rhoda worked her magic.

Most hairdressers are personable by the nature of their trade, but Rhoda also had a quality of warmth and compassion that was enveloping. She was like a loving mother hen toward her delicate customers and regarded them with honor.

She once mentioned, "I have been a professional hairdresser in various shops for most of my life, but working with the elderly, is the most rewarding job that I've ever had. They are appreciative, patient, and never complain."

Rhoda loved the residents and her work, but the cheerful smile was unable to veil a deep sadness in her eyes.

The reason was revealed to me a few weeks later, when she pensively disclosed, "My husband was diagnosed with leukemia last December and is currently undergoing chemotherapy treatments. To everyone's surprise, he's responding better than expected, but his prognosis is not good. Yesterday was a good day; he appeared stronger when old friends came for a visit, but today he's exceptionally tired, and not himself at all. Who knows about tomorrow?"

The implicit progression remained a silent thought: *If there is a tomorrow.*

I have often considered how an instant can alter a life—one diagnosis, one wrong choice, one tragic event. The world doesn't stop for those with a shattered world though, and Rhoda continued on with business as usual. She masterfully snipped the uneven ends of Dusty's hair with routine normality, but the dark circles under her eyes bespoke of many sleepless nights.

Rhoda then looked at me and shared the faith that she learned at home as a child. "My mother taught me that it's easy to say you love God, but doing the will of God is not always easy. Jesus suffered; and because we are called to follow Him, God sometimes allows suffering in our lives as well. I have committed all into His hands."

Then sweeping up before her next customer, she shrugged her shoulders and reminded me, "Life and death are ultimately in God's hands."

Chapter 10

The Unpredictable Predictable

One day, two out-of-the-ordinary occurrences took place in the dining room. The first was at breakfast, and the second at lunch. It was astonishing because everything with the residents, when it came to dining, was so predictable. Everyone sat at the same table, in the same spot and ate the same thing every morning for breakfast with one exception that I knew of: Maria alternated between a glazed donut one morning and a bagel the next. Even that, however, was predictable.

Penny sat at a table near the window adjacent to ours. She always dressed somewhat eccentrically, and brought along her morning newspaper. She emanated the aura of wealthy sophistication, and wore a diamond on her demure left hand that looked as if it was one of England's Crown Jewels.

As Jim passed by her en route to *his* table, she motioned to the waitress as if hailing a taxi and asked, "Will you please go and invite him to join me for breakfast?"

The waitress turned to look in the direction that Penny was pointing, and *invited* Jim, by taking his elbow, steering him in a sudden U-turn, and firmly saying, "Sit here."

He was slightly rattled by the twirling change of direction, but complied without protest; and Penny's whole countenance brightened as he joined her. She looked like a queen entertaining a guest and I couldn't help overhearing as she tried in vain to coerce him into conversation.

"Where did you say you were from?" she inquired with interest.

"I didn't," he responded.

After a moment of silence when she realized there would be no further elaboration, she graciously continued on about her life in New York City since 1942.

I marveled at the transformation in Penny, simply by having someone to talk to. Equally astonishing, was that Jim's total lack of social graces, or response at all for that matter, was of *no* significant importance.

At lunch, another startling event happened. Mary always dined alone while gazing out the window at the water. Unexpectedly, Ken approached Mary and asked if he could join her. We didn't learn the reason for this surprising phenomenon until the end of lunch when ninety-six-year-old Carl wheeled over to Ken and apologized sincerely for coughing while choking on a piece of food. Ken had wisely decided to move out of harm's way.

Again, I couldn't help overhearing their conversation: Mary's interest in the welfare of Ken's cat, and his response: "I don't own a cat. The cat owns me."

Ken then took the helm by stating, "New York is much more than just a city you know; it's actually five boroughs."

This eye-opener did not impress Mary who is from upstate New York. She retorted sarcastically, "Did *you know* that New York is more than a city with five boroughs—it's actually a state?"

When dessert was served, Mary commented on how sloppy the cake was. She repeated three or four times to Ken, "You have to admit, this sure is a sloppy cake!"

Ken, still out of sorts, steadfastly stood his ground and refused to admit to anything. When Mary finally took a bite, she said with surprise, "This is pretty good, sloppy and all."

Ken, determining that a response was finally warranted, irritably asked, "Which part? The part that you succeeded in getting into your mouth or the part that you picked up off of your lap?"

Chapter 11

Janette

One morning as I took Dusty to the dining room for breakfast, I was stopped by a dear resident named John, who was headed back to his room. Shaking his head, he asked me, "Have you heard about Janette?"

"No," I replied.

He informed me that she was dying, gave me her room number, and said, "You need to go see her."

It was spoken in such a matter-of-fact manner, that he hardly broke his unsteady stride as he continued out of the dining room. To me, however, the impact of his words came like a punch in the stomach and I thought back to when I had first met her.

Janette came to Bridgeport a few weeks after I arrived. She was comparatively alert and vibrant, and would at times join us on the porch. I watched as her children lovingly helped her settle in, and took turns visiting.

When she immediately lost the new cell phone that she had just been given, they patiently coached her with the replacement. "You hold it like this, Mom. Now push this button to answer."

Her distinguishing feature was a strong New York accent, which personified that she had once been a "pretty tough cookie."

Janette's condition brought me face to face with the "end of life" questions that confront families. Advance directives? The heartbreaking decisions to discontinue further medical treatment... When to stop medications? When to resuscitate? When to pull a plug?

Janette was no longer able to tolerate dialysis, and the treatment was discontinued, with its inevitable results. She was brought back to Bridgeport, from the hospital, to die. For virtually twenty-four hours a day, Janette's children took turns at her side, and when I went to visit as John had suggested, I saw a woman in bed who would not be getting back up. I quietly sat next to her and held her hand, praying that God would receive her peacefully into His arms and comfort her family.

I thought about how fleeting and fragile life is, recalling Psalm 90:12, "Lord, teach us to number our days, that we may apply our hearts to wisdom," and asked Him for the wisdom to prioritize our priorities.

She passed away a few days later.

For loved ones left behind, death is a grievous blow, and I was struck again by the pain that it brings.

Chapter 12

Valentine's Day 2013

Valentine's Day at Bridgeport meant a party with excited preparations beginning early in the day. The celebration began at 6:30 in the evening and was complete with decorations, food, punch (spiked and un-spiked), and live music.

What made this evening so special was that a group of midshipmen came from the Naval Academy to spend Valentine's Day with the elderly. I have never seen a group of finer young people. They were immaculately dressed in full uniform, and the women's uniform included skirts with nylons and black patent leather pumps. Two things stood out, besides their impeccable appearance and polite, respectful manner: one was the way that they intermingled with the residents. When I arrived, Dusty was seated between a young man and woman, and was gaily chatting away. This scene was replicated throughout the room. Their interaction looked effortless, spontaneous, and natural. It was a delight to see.

Second, the midshipmen danced with the residents. The entertainment and buffet was set up in the dining room, and this was where the party began, complete with food, dancing, and laughter.

One old gentleman in particular gave the young ladies a run for their money while trying to teach them the "jitter-bug." He would dance with one partner at a time confidently twirling them around, and upon finishing, the girls were flush-faced and out of breath.

Another resident named Pam was the surprise of the evening. She always carried herself with quiet reserve and grace. As a fun-loving young man escorted Pam to the dance floor, she was transformed into a youthful "dancing machine." She led her head-bobbing, finger-snapping partner into a

"Boogie-Woogie" as though they were at a sock hop in the 1950s.

For the other residents who were less mobile, these midshipmen expressed a caring thoughtfulness that was touching. They held hands and swayed with those in wheel chairs, and took small steps with those who could stand.

The young man who had been sitting with Dusty when I first arrived approached our table later and asked, "Dusty, would you like to dance?"

He already knew her name from before, and when he lifted her up from the wheelchair, he looked at me and promised, "I won't let her fall."

He gently held her close, moving slowly to the music until the song was over. Then placing her back in her wheelchair, he took her hand in his, bowed graciously and said, "Thank you for the dance."

It was a magical evening that turned back the pages of time to a simpler, kinder, and more respectful era. How remarkable that these young servicemen and women would spend this "holiday of love" with the elderly, at a nursing home facility.

Chapter 13

The Men's Table

Fenton, Calvin, Austin, and Monty are four aged gentlemen new to Bridgeport. Their table was also neighboring ours and I briefly chatted with each of them during our comings and goings at breakfast. Monty was a professor at prestigious university near Annapolis for over fifty years, and three out of the four were World War II veterans. All of them had presence of mind, albeit in a state of decline, nonetheless. They had a wonderful camaraderie with one another, as they politely discussed the latest world events, politics, and sports over pancakes and coffee.

The fact that they clearly understood their present diminished condition was notable, not only because most residents don't, but also because for the most part, their banter back and forth was lighthearted and amusing. They would commiserate with a chuckle on how incredibly *far away* Annapolis had become.

"I'm deaf in one ear and can't hear out of the other," Cal lamented, continuing his complaint further by adding, "You have things and can't use them."

"I know, my car just sits there," Fenton sighed.

Austin then piped in, "I gave mine to my niece."

Austin, who was ninety-one years old, then proceeded to share his war experiences with his fascinated buddies.

"I was ambushed and captured during the legendary Battle of the Bulge."

It was a story that he re-told with incredible detail, shaking his head at the painful memory, of the atrocities that he both saw and endured.

"I remained a prisoner of war in the German camp for four months until General Patton and his men rescued the American POWs toward the end of the War. I love that man!" he exclaimed with reverence.

Then, suddenly, as if awakening from the past and returning to the present, he continued, "I remember it like it was yesterday, and what happened yesterday, I can't remember!"

With chagrin, the other three acknowledged, this last statement applied to all of them.

Then downing the last sip of coffee, they slowly dispersed back to their rooms to read, nap, or watch a ball game. The lurking enemies now were boredom and loneliness; and visits from family were the welcomed rescue.

Chapter 14

Sara turned 100 years old on August 17, 2013 and I was invited to the party. She was dressed in a baby blue polyester pantsuit with a corsage pinned on her shoulder and surrounded by her loved ones, she simply glowed. The Activities Director took charge of the occasion by reading a summary of her extraordinary personal history, followed by two letters. The first letter was from the mayor of Annapolis proclaiming August 17 to be known henceforth as "Sara Bloom Day!"

The second was from the Baltimore Orioles, thanking her for being a faithful fan for so many years.

After listening to the lengthy accolades being read, she got directly to the point "Did they enclose any tickets?"

The party continued with loving comments from her family and friends. Although a widow now, Sara had been married for over half a century and they had raised three sons together.

When one of her sons took the microphone, he laughingly quipped, "Even though I'm over seventy years old, she *still* tells me what to do!"

The director concluded the celebration by serving a beautiful cake. She apologized for not putting a hundred candles on it because of the fire hazard and Sara retorted, "It's just as well. I'd probably have a heart attack trying to blow them all out."

Laughter filled the room and we all sang "Happy Birthday" to this remarkable woman.

Sara and I had become friends six months earlier, when she first came to Bridgeport and joined our table. She had a strong, independent personality with vestiges of a tall, lean, athletic build. Even though Sara was legally blind and wore hearing aids in both ears, she walked easily with a cane and still possessed all of her mental faculties. This was immediately discernable upon meeting her. She was the only resident that I knew of who came to Bridgeport of her own volition. After breaking her hip in January, Sara determined *it was time*. She sold her home and all of the antiques that she had acquired through the years, and hardly looked back.

At mealtime, Sara would often lift her eyes in exasperation, and sometimes with sadness, as she observed the varying stages of dementia around her. It was glaring, even to someone with limited vision. She would shake her head in disbelief at the numerous spills or the irrational peculiarities, such as when Maria would pour packets of sugar over her food unless I gently intervened.

Without realizing it, however, Sara contributed to the oddities of our table as well. She would hand me her menu in a commanding fashion, and ask, "Would you please read this to me? I can't make out what it says."

"Sure," I replied; initially unaware the simple request would become a mildly embarrassing, *daily* broadcast. On a volume scale of one to five, I progressively escalated until shouting at a category five, before she understood me well enough to make her decision. By the time she finally arrived at that point, my throat felt slightly hoarse and the *entire building* had heard, at peak decibel, the menu options for the day.

What amazed me the most about Sara was her insightfulness. She often commented about my care for Dusty as she observed us together and frequently told me the reason Dusty was doing so well was because of love. I marveled that someone who was 100 years old, nearly deaf, and legally blind, could *see* so clearly.

Chapter 15

I first met Helen not because I saw her, but because I *heard* her. She was sitting in the parlor one afternoon singing, "Surely the presence of the Lord is in this place," as if she and the Lord were the only ones in the room. Remarkable was not only the fact that she loved to sing and would sing anytime, anywhere regardless of who was around her, but once introduced, Helen would remember everyone's name.

I discovered this fact a few days after I met her, when I reminded her of mine.

"I know who you are!" she replied in an almost-offended-matter-of-fact manner, as if a good memory was the *norm* in this assisted-living facility. When I asked her, "How are you able to remember everyone's name with just one introduction?" Her response was spontaneous and clear-cut, "Because they're all precious to me."

Dusty and I would stop and talk with Helen whenever I saw her and occasionally, I would visit with her in her room while Dusty napped. At the end of every visit, she would sing to me before I left. Her voice was ordinary, but the uninhibited, heartfelt manner in which she sang was not; it always moved me in an unexplainable way.

One morning after breakfast, as we were about to leave the dining room, Helen motioned for me to come over and asked, "Do you want to hear a new song?"

Nodding my head, I stooped beside her and held her hand. Oblivious to those around us, she instructed me to close my eyes as she sang, "The Lord knows the way through the wilderness, all you have to do is follow." Her eyes had a joyful shine in them and I left the bustling dining room transported on the same cloud that she was on.

Later that day, she invited me to come to her room the following afternoon for a visit. I went while Dusty was sleeping, and discovered Helen was sick in bed. It was a shock to see her without her wig on because she was nearly bald, and it was the first thing that she asked as I approached, "Anne, would you please hand me my hair?"

I handed her the wig from a stand on the dresser, and while adjusting it, she continued, "I haven't been able to eat anything all day. Will you sit with me? I don't want to be alone."

"Of course," I said, but before sitting down, I retrieved some ginger ale from her refrigerator and encouraged her to try to drink some of it.

While she sipped from a straw that I held for her, she quietly asked, "Will you be my daughter?"

I looked at her tenderly and softly answered, "Yes, you can have me."

Soon after that, she lay back on the pillow with a tired sigh and asked, "Would you sing to me?"

I sat on the bed, holding this dear woman's hand, and sang to her.

After nearly an hour, I went back to Dusty's room, promising to return later. When I arrived back, with soup and crackers in hand, a caregiver was near Helen's door in the hallway and explained she was being transported to the hospital. As the paramedics carried her out of the room on a gurney, she looked at me and weakly said, "I love you, Anne."

Helen died two days later.

Chapter 16

The Sin of Indifference

When I arrived at Bridgeport on Wednesday, August 7, 2014, Dusty was in her wheelchair in her pajama bottoms and bra. The smell of urine was strong as I entered the room, and it became apparent that both Dusty and the bed were soaking wet. She was agitated and couldn't tell me what had happened, but I wondered who had gotten her up and had left her sitting alone and confused in that condition with the door wide open. Deeply troubled, I determined to investigate and address the matter later.

"Why don't we get ready for breakfast?" I softly suggested.

I tried to help her stand, but she cried out in pain, so I gently lowered her to the floor, pressing the emergency button for help. After a few minutes, one of the staff members came and immediately called for an ambulance. I then learned Dusty had fallen out of bed shortly before I arrived. After a brief examination, the on-duty med-tech and care-giver had mistakenly determined she wasn't hurt and plunked her soaking wet in her wheelchair to wait until I arrived later. I was angered by the carelessness.

Indifference is like an insidious, invasive species that takes root for a number of reasons. It often grows unawares, drains a person of vitality, and hardens them over time. Calloused indifference generally breeds negligence and I suspected this was the case now.

I put a pillow under Dusty's head and held her until the paramedics arrived. As they entered the room and began to examine her, Dusty's petite stature and feisty personality became evident. When the burly paramedic commented she was a tough little lady, Dusty wanted to prove the point by asking, "Do you want me to hit you?"

We all laughed as he replied, "You'll have to get in line for that one! There's a lot of people ahead of you that want to do that."

Standing in the doorway, another EMT went through the list of Dusty's allergies, and quizzically announced, "It says here that she's allergic to God?"

The others piped up in unison, "Allergic to God? Never heard of that one before. That can't be right. *That's what it says?*"

Standing next to him, I politely plucked the paper from his hand and asked, "May I see that? It says she's allergic to *cod*, the fish!"

The seriousness of the situation was lightened by their kindness and sense of humor, but they too, were angered at the inefficiency that they witnessed.

The lead EMT sternly scolded the staff nurse on duty saying, "You need to have the resident's medical information legible and in order; you have no answers for *anything* we've asked you!"

They then took Dusty to the hospital in the ambulance and I followed behind in my car. I checked in at the desk and waited in the Emergency Room until I was allowed to go back with her.

At the hospital, x-rays revealed Dusty had in fact broken her hip. I was in constant communication with Nina for information and decisions, as she was out of town at the time. A partial hip replacement was done later in the day, and the surgery went well. After four days in the hospital, which for me were emotionally grueling, Dusty was transferred to a rehabilitation center for two weeks, and then to Creekside Assisted Living, which had a specialized memory care unit.

Chapter 17

Transition

The rehabilitation center was a time of convalescence and the care was exceptional. The doctors, nurses, and staff were attentive and helpful. They were thorough in monitoring Dusty's progress and did everything possible to ensure her comfort. Physical therapy was a prescribed part of her recovery treatment. Although the therapist made a valiant effort, Dusty was unable to comprehend enough to actively participate; therefore, it was discontinued after a few sessions.

On one particularly hectic afternoon toward the end of her stay, Dusty had become agitated by the bustling activity, prodding, and questions. In the midst of the commotion around us, I sat down next to her on the bed without saying a word, and quietly held her hand.

Suddenly, it was as if everything in the background faded, when Dusty looked at me earnestly and asked, "Do you love me?"

Her question stunned me, and with tears welling up in my eyes, I answered, "Yes, I love you."

Then she inquired further, "Truly?"

Looking at her intently, I responded, "I *truly* love you," and laid my head on her shoulder.

She put her arms around me and replied, "I truly love you too."

I wept as I realized the one level that Dusty could not only genuinely relate to, but still *communicate* in a real, meaningful way, was love. It was a rare and precious moment that I will never forget.

After two weeks, Dusty was transferred to Creekside and the transition to the new facility went well. Her physical recovery was surprisingly pain-free, but the dementia was steadily gaining ground. Nina had decorated Dusty's new room with cheerful colors, family mementos, and pictures, but the familiar photos no longer sparked recognition or memory. Dusty was sleeping more, and oblivious to her new surroundings or that the move had even taken place.

Creekside had two sections. One side of the building was designated for assisted living and the other side of the building was the memory care unit (MCU). The MCU differed from assisted living, in that admittance was based on diminished cognitive level and it was a secured, safe environment, offering complete care for those who were severely impaired. Activities were designed to strengthen both mental and physical health and were held in the main room. The dining room was adjacent to that and the residents were assigned to tables according to compatibility. Each resident had a private room and bath, but the lines of personal space and property were often blurred. Other than naps, outings, and family visits, the residents spent the days together in one area or the other, with monitored care.

Initially, I missed the picturesque view of the bay at Bridgeport, but Creekside had an enclosed outdoor courtyard with porch swings and raised garden beds. The beautiful gardens created a homelike atmosphere where the residents could pick the vegetables and flowers at will, as if they were in their own backyard. It was a wonderful concept and much time was spent there when the weather was nice.

Once again, Dusty and I settled into a normal daily routine. Three regular meals were provided, with activities and snacks in between. We participated in the activities and outings as much as possible, but she had become unmindful of most of it.

Being together is what made a difference now; in fact, at this stage, being together is what made the *all* the difference.

Chapter 18

Sunshine Through the Haze

D uring our days at Creekside, Dusty and I sat together near the others during activities and meals. Although the "fog" was denser and more difficult to navigate with the MCU residents, there were still occasional lucid moments and memories that surfaced from beneath layers of forgetfulness. Personalities, emotions, and the ability to form friendships were severely altered, but not altogether eliminated. I once again began to both see and appreciate what was left.

Mr. Clark was an endearing "old school" gentleman. On outings, he would help those who were less mobile, and hold the door for everyone. He referred to himself as an "old country boy," but Mr. Clark had once been a brilliant engineer, with a hobby of beekeeping.

He would discuss the engineering wonder and design of the honeycomb in its hexagonal perfection, and ask me, "Did you know that honeybees use the sun as a compass in navigation?"

Without waiting for an answer, he'd continue, "It's how they find their way back to the hive."

He would tell this to me repeatedly, each time as though it was the first, and I would marvel repeatedly, each time.

Mr. Johnston was *not* a gentleman of any sort. He was a crusty, but good-natured police officer who had worked in Baltimore until he retired. I would overhear him in the dining room, as he would tell off-color jokes and stories from his years on the streets that kept everyone laughing. He also told of the emergency calls at all hours of the night, where he raced to save many from desperate situations. The one thing that he never mentioned was his bravery.

In spite of the fact that many of the residents' conversations were often nonsensical and without pause or punctuation, the relationships that developed were genuine. They not only formed friendships among each other, but they bonded with staff. One of the most poignant examples of this was the bond that formed between Mama and Frank.

Mama was a diminutive woman with large arthritic hands that looked bigger than she was. I don't even remember her name, because *everyone* referred to her as "Mama." Mama loved Frank, a young maintenance man who had worked there many years. Frank always had a big smile on his face and a loud contagious laugh. When he would laugh, which was often, it was like opening the window and letting in sunshine and fresh air. Every time he walked through the MCU, Mama would motion for him to come over with her crooked bony index finger. Frank would always take time to go over to where she was sitting in her wheel-chair, squat down to eye level, and spend a few moments with her before returning to the task at hand. Sometimes, he would take her outside and sit with her when the weather was nice. Her face would light up whenever she saw him.

One Monday morning, I arrived back to work and Mama was gone. She had passed away over the weekend and a cloud of sadness hung over the MCU. Later that morning, I bumped into Frank as I was getting a cup of tea in the kitchenette for staff and residents. His perennial cheerfulness was overshadowed by the genuine sense of loss that he felt.

Looking into his solemn eyes, I simply said to him, "She loved you."

He silently nodded, before returning to work.

What was surprising was the bond that was formed in spite of Mama's severe limited cognitive function and almost complete lack of verbal expression. What was surprising was not what Frank meant to Mama, but what Mama had come to mean to Frank.

Chapter 19

Devotion

In our increasingly self-centered world, the promise to stand beside someone in "sickness or in health," are words that are idly spoken, in vows that are seldom kept. At Creekside, however, I observed the antithesis of this. I discovered true devotion, born of love and tested by time and hardship. This precious gem was found in spouses caring for the other one with dementia. Their love and commitment had grown through the years. Now, hours were spent with loved ones who barely recognized them, day after day, month after month, year after year. What made their devotion all the more radiant, was that they were unmindful of the rare quality they possessed. It reminded me of Moses returning from Mount Sinai, completely unaware his face was shining.

One case was a husband's early onset of Alzheimer's. I became acquainted with his wife when he first arrived at Creekside and she shared with me, "My husband was in his fifties and intuitively knew something was wrong before anyone else. He told me prior to the confirmed diagnosis, in order to prepare me for the hard road ahead."

In a different situation, the husband's brain damage was the result of a medical error during a minor surgery.

"My husband's brain was deprived of oxygen during the procedure and the damage was irreparable. The husband that I knew, died that day," she told me over lunch one afternoon.

Yet, her love was unfailing and she was devotedly at his side for hours, every day.

Another instance was a decorated World War II veteran tending to his wife. We sat together at the same table in the dining room and I watched as he made sure that all of her needs were met, while being in poor health himself.

Dementia is tragic at any age, but the early onset of this erosive disease is heart-rending beyond words. The costly jewel of devotion in those at Creekside was found in a mine of deep hardship.

Chapter 20

"The Golden Rule"

Surprisingly, the aesthetics of a building, the programs offered, and the expense of a facility does not necessarily equate to quality care. Quality care in a facility involves many people and it depends upon the compassion, sensitivity, and training of the individual who is directly handling the patient *at that time*. Med-techs and caregivers change with each shift and staff can become skeletal for any number of reasons. One person may be skilled and compassionate and another may be less proficient. The truth is, levels of care can vary at *any* facility at *any* given time. Family involvement is crucial in this concerted effort, because family is the *heart* of care.

"The Golden Rule"—do unto others as you would have them do unto you—is the simplicity of kindness that kept me from ever taking a shortcut. I tried to care for Dusty the same way that I would want to be cared for, should our positions be reversed. Although it has been said "nothing is certain in life but death and taxes," there are other universal certainties: We are *all* getting older, and we *all* need the help of others at various times in life. Dementia/Alzheimer's has reached epidemic proportions in this country and no one is immune from potentially needing the care of someone else in the future. "The Golden Rule" is a guiding principle of consideration toward others that sets the bar for high quality care.

Chapter 21

Discovering Gold

B eing at Bridgeport and Creekside reminded me of how I felt when my youngest was an infant and I had to return to work.

I would tell the babysitter, "You ought to be paying me for the privilege of keeping my child!"

I said it in a joking manner and we would laugh, but in my heart, I meant it. After dropping off my precious bundle, I would cry on my way to work, pretending to have allergies once I arrived so that no one would know.

I felt the same way with Dusty and the other residents. Spending the day with the elderly is a *privilege,* and as I mentioned before, it is like discovering gold. Gold is a precious substance that is not readily noticeable. It's hidden in the earth and you have to look for it. Beneath the weakness, frailty, and varying stages of dementia lies a hidden vast array of wealth.

Kathryn spoke of it so aptly, "These people have lived through times of war and peace. Many had come through the Great Depression as children where the difficulties were so dire that the motto of the day was, 'Brother, can you spare a dime?'"

Their lives are rich with experiences, wisdom and humor, but you have to take the time to listen.

Really listen.

If you do, your life is enriched.

Chapter 22

The Power of Touch

On Sunday morning May 1, 2016, Dusty was transported to the hospital by ambulance because she had become increasingly unresponsive. She had deteriorated to the point that she was no longer eating, and I would have to hold her head up with one hand, while simultaneously holding a can of Ensure to her lips with the other. It would take nearly forty-five minutes of miniscule sips by rote on her part and considerable effort on mine for her to finish one small can. Ensure had started off as a dietary supplement to regular meals, but gradually became the sole source of nourishment as her appetite declined. It was not enough however, and Dusty was not only losing weight, but she also became dehydrated.

In the Emergency Room, the doctor took some tests and ordered an IV to rehydrate her. He then gently gave us the grim prognosis: Dusty was in the final stages of dementia with about two weeks to live. After conferring with Nina, he placed her on Comfort Care, which meant that all meals and prior medications would be stopped.

Dusty would be given only what was necessary to keep her comfortable, including morphine if needed. She was then transferred back to Creekside under the supervision of hospice; a team of end-of-life specialists that not only monitored her condition, but also advised us on what to expect. Nina and I became a "tag team" of sorts, going back and forth to the MCU every couple of hours to give Dusty as much nutrition and hydration as possible. We would mix baby cereal into her Ensure, pureed vegetables into juice drinks, yogurt into smoothies, and change her position frequently in order to reduce the possibility of bedsores. Hydration was the key and Dusty did improve slightly, but we both knew ultimately, this was a battle we could not win.

During this time, I made a profound discovery about the power of touch. One day after feeding Dusty, I scooted her over on the hospital bed so that we could sit next to each other as we always had. There was something in her shrunken body that appeared to come alive as *she* drew closer to me and put her head on my shoulder. Even though Dusty and I had spent most of our days together like this, on a love seat in the activities room, or on a porch swing outside, it was the first time that I recognized the power of touch. She *responded* to it, when she had little or no response to anything else.

We are born with five senses: sight, hearing, smell, taste, and touch. Touch compensates when mental acuity declines and the other senses diminish, because it bypasses them and makes a connection when all else fails.

As infants, we are nurtured and held. It's crucial to our development, but what I didn't realize is that it's equally important with the aged. Touch is a manifestation of love that keeps us from feeling alone and abandoned. We need to hold our elderly.

Dusty died the night of June 28, 2016, with Nina camped at her bedside.

Note to the Reader:

The names of both assisted living facilities and of the residents have been changed in order to respect privacy. My intention is not to find fault or criticize in anyway because caregiving is challenging; having a loved one with dementia is challenging; and operating an assisted living facility is challenging. I have the utmost admiration and respect for those involved with the care of others. It is a collaborative effort and most do an incredible job.

My initial purpose in writing this short memoir was for my own personal journal and to share with immediate family. My sister encouraged me to publish it, however, because she believed that my experiences would enable others to see beyond their outward loss. What remains when mental function declines or when verbal communication is no longer possible? What's left when your parent or spouse no longer recognizes you, when their reasoning capability is non-existent or their personality has been severely altered? Love remains.

It's futile to try to hold on to what is no longer there, but love reaches beyond reason and meaningful bonds that transcend limitations are *still* reciprocal and *can* be embraced. It may appear visiting doesn't matter because a loved one won't remember you came or recognize you, but I didn't know Dusty prior to the disease and she *never* knew my name or recognized me, per se; nonetheless, there was a special bond between us and I was as much the beneficiary of our time together as she was.

Only love can grieve. I grieved when Dusty died and I miss her. It was an experience that I will cherish forever.

Acknowledgments

To Jesus:
My all in all.

To my children:
Moses, Sharon, Daniel, and Rachel
The "cords have never been cut"
because of our unbreakable bonds of love.

To my sister, Christine:
This book would *not* have happened
without your faith and support.

To Tom and Nina:
My life has been enriched
because you opened your hearts and home to me
and encouraged me to try new things.

To Jim and Dawn:
Jim had a special place in Dusty's heart,
and always made her laugh.

To the rest of my family:
Thank you for your steadfast love
through thick and thin.

and

To Taylor Graham:
My editor and coach.

CPSIA information can be obtained
at www.ICGtesting.com
Printed in the USA
LVHW051505080419
613378LV00017B/676/P